I0794703

1

Crisis in Eschatology

MESSAGE OVERVIEW

A. Introduction to Eschatology

1. Eschatology is the subdivision of systematic theology that is particularly concerned with the last days.
2. Among Christians there is very little consensus on the topic of eschatology.
3. The crisis in our time is the problem of understanding biblical prophecy.
4. There are a number of big eschatological issues that are debated among Christians, including: the time and nature of the Millennium, the identity of the Antichrist, the time of the Rapture, and the relationship between the church and Israel.

B. The Most Serious Crisis of Eschatology

1. The question of the credibility of the Bible and of Jesus Himself.
2. For 200 years there has been an unprecedented assault against the trustworthiness of Scripture both inside and outside the church.
3. The number one point of attack of the higher critics against inspiration focuses upon matters related to eschatology.
    a. Two thirds of the New Testament deals with future prophecy.
    b. If that prophecy is suspect, serious questions about the nature and credibility of the Bible are raised.
4. More serious is the attack against the credibility of Christ Himself.
    a. The critics claim that Jesus' prophecies did not come to pass within the specific time frame that He Himself said they would.
    b. If this criticism is true, it would reduce Jesus to a false prophet.
5. The problem illustrated — Bertrand Russell's *Why I Am Not a Christian*
    a. Russell outlines a series of criticisms focused upon Jesus.
    b. He claims that although the Christ of the Gospels displays a high moral character, he does not display a great deal of wisdom, especially in his teaching about the future.

   c. According to Russell, Jesus certainly thought that His second coming would occur in clouds of glory before the death of the people who were living at that time.
   d. This is the chief criticism of Russell, and it has been the chief criticism of biblical critics for the last 200 years.
6. There are three primary texts to which critics point:
   a. Matthew 10:23
   b. Matthew 16:28
   c. Mark 13:30
7. The manner in which evangelical scholars have handled these time texts has in many cases been far less than satisfying.
8. There are numerous statements in the New Testament indicating that the early church had a sense of urgency about the nearness or imminence of the coming of Christ, yet these things have not occurred even to this day.
9. Critics claim that as time passed the early church made certain adjustments to its expectations, which appear in the later books of the New Testament.
10. The primary concern of this series of messages will be to understand the scriptural time-frame references that people have used to criticize the credibility of the Bible and the credibility of our Lord Himself.

STUDY QUESTIONS

1. What is the meaning of the term "eschatology"?

2. What is the most serious crisis in eschatology today?

3. Name the two persons or things whose credibility is challenged by higher critics.

4. When attacking the inspiration of Scripture, what is the number one point of attack of higher critics?

5. What is the specific complaint critics raise concerning the credibility of Christ?

6. Why is this criticism significant?

7. Why did Bertrand Russell claim that Christ did not display a great deal of wisdom?

8. What are the three main texts cited by critics to establish their attack upon the prophecies of Christ?

9. What is the theory of the higher critics concerning the eschatological expectation of the early church?

STUDY GUIDE

The Last Days According to Jesus

R.C. Sproul

LIGONIER MINISTRIES
Renew your Mind.
LIGONIER.ORG | 800-435-4343

421 Ligonier Court, Sanford, FL 32771
E-mail: info@ligonier.org

Printed in China.

DISCUSSION QUESTIONS

1. How important do you believe the study of eschatology to be? Why?
2. There is a large amount of disagreement among Christians on the doctrines of eschatology. Are these disagreements significant enough to justify division in the church? Why or why not?
3. Are there any eschatological doctrines or theories that would place a person outside the boundaries of orthodox Christianity? Explain.
4. Examine the three texts of Scripture cited by the higher critics to disprove the prophecies of Jesus. How have you heard these texts explained? Do you find these explanations satisfactory? Why or why not?

2

Understanding the Parousia

MESSAGE OVERVIEW

A. Introduction — Need for Historical Reconnaissance of Critical Theories

B. Nineteenth Century Theology

1. The philosophy of the nineteenth century was influenced by Hegel and his evolutionary view of history.
2. Evolutionary philosophy was applied by biblical scholars to the development of religion.
3. The Religious Historical School that arose from this dominated nineteenth century liberal theology. According to this school, biblical religion follows the same basic pattern that all religions follow in their historical development, by moving from the simple to the complex.
4. Alongside the Religious Historical School's application of evolutionary principles to the development of biblical religion was a powerful anti-super-natural bias that controlled the analysis of Scripture and created a crisis in the church.
5. Liberalism revised Christianity to make it compatible with modern theories about man and the world.
6. The kingdom of God motif that unified the Old Testament and the New Testament was redefined in terms of ethics and values.

C Albrecht Ritschl

1. He argued that the teaching of Jesus must not be understood in supernatural terms of personal salvation but rather in terms of important human values.
2. The kingdom of God has to do with social application of the ethical teaching of Jesus.
3. His views would later give rise to the "social gospel" of Walter Rauschenbusch.
4. Ever since Ritschl there has been a cleavage between the liberal and conservative understanding of the basic mission of the church.

D. Albert Schweitzer

1. His book, *The Quest for the Historical Jesus*, which was published in the early twentieth century, made a huge impact on biblical studies.
2. He analyzed and critiqued the evolutionary thought of nineteenth-century liberalism and its revision of the kingdom of God concept.
3. He argued that the message of Jesus about the kingdom of God is unintelligible apart from the central focus of eschatology.
4. According to Schweitzer, the kingdom does not come by a gradual, evolutionary, this-worldly, progressive development of ethics; instead, it will come catastrophically and suddenly from above.
5. According to Schweitzer, there were different points in Jesus' ministry when he expected the sudden breakthrough of the kingdom of heaven, such as Luke 10, and Matthew 21 and 26.
6. On the cross, Jesus finally realizes it isn't going to happen, cries out, "My God, My God, Why have you forsaken me?" (Matt. 27:46), and dies a noble figure who embodied the Gospel of love.
7. The value of Schweitzer — It is now impossible to ignore the eschatological language of the New Testament.
8. The problem with Schweitzer — He believed Jesus was wrong.

E. C.H. Dodd

1. Dodd developed what is now termed "realized eschatology," which means that the predictions of Jesus for the most part refer to the first century.
2. Jesus was not disillusioned, and the time-frame references did not fail to materialize but were fulfilled in a spiritual sense.
3. The disciples did see the kingdom of God being manifested because the very presence of Jesus was a manifestation of the kingdom.

F. Oscar Cullmann

1. He developed a theory based upon an analogy with D-day.
2. Just as D-day signaled the end of the conflict, the first coming saw the decisive coming of the kingdom of God.
3. All that is left is the postscript at the end of history, V-E Day.

G. Herman Ridderbos

1. He developed the concept of the "already/not-yet" coming of the kingdom of God.
2. The kingdom has "already" come in large measure, but there still remains at the end of time the final consummation of that kingdom.

STUDY QUESTIONS

1. What theory dominated nineteenth century theological thinking?
2. According to the nineteenth century Religious Historical School, what process of development did biblical religion follow?
3. How was the kingdom of God redefined by liberalism?
4. How did Albrecht Ritschl redefine the teaching of Jesus?
5. What late nineteenth century movement did Ritschl's thought give rise to?
6. How do conservatives and liberals differ in their view of the basic mission of the church?
7. What was the name of the early twentieth century book that had a dramatic impact on biblical studies about the kingdom of God?
8. What important contribution did Albert Schweitzer make to biblical studies?
9. What is the meaning of the term "parousia delay"?

DISCUSSION QUESTIONS

1. How did nineteenth–century liberalism choose to handle the crisis caused by the Religious Historical School and the widespread anti-supernatural bias of the era?
2. Summarize the eschatological views of Albert Schweitzer, C.H. Dodd, Oscar Cullmann, and Herman Ridderbos.
3. Dispensationalism attempted to solve the nineteenth century crisis by placing the fulfillment of all New Testament prophecy at the end of history. Does this solution do justice to the language of the New Testament? Why or why not?
4. Do any of the solutions discussed thus far deal adequately with all of the scriptural teaching? Explain.

3

A Question of Time

MESSAGE OVERVIEW

A. Introduction — One of the Main Problems in Prophetic Interpretation is the Question of Genre

B. The Importance of the Olivet Discourse
   1. It is the chief target of biblical critics.
   2. The main thread of the discourse follows the normal didactic pattern of language found elsewhere in the Gospels.
   3. It is contained in all three of the synoptic Gospels (Matt. 24, Mark 13, and Luke 21).

C. An Overview of the Olivet Discourse (Mark 13)
   1. Jesus' initial prophecy (vv. 1–2).
      a. At this point the disciples are on their way out of the temple complex heading toward the Mount of Olives on the other side of the valley.
      b. A great irony here is that the fulfillment of future prophecies is one of the main tools used to defend the authority of the Bible, and here we have a prophecy (the destruction of Jerusalem and the temple) that was fulfilled about 40 years after the prophecy was spoken.
      c. At the time Jesus said these things, the destruction of Jerusalem and the temple was absolutely unthinkable.
   2. The disciples ask two questions (vv. 3–4).
      a. "When will these things be?"
      b. "What will be the sign when all these things will be fulfilled?"
   3. Signs of the times (vv. 5–8).
      a. Jesus speaks of a number of preliminary signs.
      b. This is in response to the disciples' second question.
   4. Further signs (vv. 9–13).
      a. We usually assume that the primary audience here is us, but here Jesus is answering a specific question by specific people.

   b. Again and again, Jesus emphasizes the word "you" as He speaks to the disciples.
5. The Abomination of Desolation and Great Tribulation (vv. 14–20).
   a. Most contemporary interpreters assume that this prophecy refers to events in our future, but Jesus gives the disciples to whom He is speaking specific instructions concerning how to escape these events.
   b. In AD 70, as the Jews fled to Jerusalem to escape the Roman armies, the Christians fled to the hills.
6. Signs in heaven and the coming of the Son of Man (vv. 21–27).
   a. Jesus clearly includes this element of the prophecy as part of the same answer to the disciples' specific question referring to the destruction of Jerusalem and the temple.
   b. It is also included in the "all these things" that must be fulfilled before "this generation" passes away.
   c. Included in this single future prophecy, however, is not only the destruction of Jerusalem and the temple but also His coming at the end of the age on clouds of glory.

D. Several Solutions have been Proposed to this Difficult Text
   1. The biblical critics — Jesus was simply wrong.
   2. The majority of evangelicalism — Interprets the elements of the prophecy literally but spiritualizes the term "this generation" to refer to something other than the generation to whom Jesus was speaking.
   3. The minority viewpoint — Interprets "this generation" literally and understands the "coming" to be the coming of Christ in judgment at the end of the Jewish age.

STUDY QUESTIONS

1. What is one of the primary difficulties involved in the interpretation of biblical prophecy?

2. What are some of the characteristics of apocalyptic literature?

3. What are the three reasons the Olivet discourse is important in any study of eschatology?

4. In what three New Testament chapters is the Olivet discourse found?

5. Why is it ironic that biblical critics focus upon the Olivet discourse in their attacks upon New Testament prophecy?

6. What is the approximate year that the discourse was spoken by Jesus?

7. When were Jerusalem and the temple destroyed by the Roman armies?

8. What is the context of the disciples' question in Mark 13:3–4?

9. What are the two specific questions the disciples ask Jesus in Mark 13:4?

10. To whom is Jesus primarily speaking in Mark 13?

11. What is the difficulty raised in Mark 13:21–27 in relation to the earlier statements in Mark 13:1–20?

12. What are three of the methods Christians have used to handle this difficulty?

DISCUSSION QUESTIONS

1. Read the three accounts of the Olivet discourse (Matt. 24, Mark 13, Luke 21). What do the accounts have in common? In what ways do the accounts differ in their emphasis and in the specific details they reveal?
2. Why is the immediate context of the Olivet discourse so important to its correct interpretation? Explain.
3. Of the common approaches to the Olivet discourse, which do you affirm? What are the strengths of this approach? What are the weaknesses? What are the strengths and weaknesses of the approaches you do not affirm?

4

Literal or Figurative?

MESSAGE OVERVIEW

A. Introduction — Review of Mark 13

B. The Interpretation of the Olivet Discourse

1. The first thing to deal with is our basic principle of interpretation — the *sensus literalis* — the literal sense of Scripture.
   a. The popular understanding of "literal" is that it means things take place in exactly the way they are described in Scripture.
   b. The actual meaning of the concept is that the Bible is to be interpreted in the sense in which it was written — poetry is interpreted as poetry, history as history, figurative language as figurative language.
2. In interpreting the Olivet discourse, we must distinguish between ordinary and figurative language.
   a. Ordinary — The text means exactly what it seems to say in the ordinary use of language.
   b. Figurative — The text includes a symbolic element.
3. Three basic options in interpreting the Olivet discourse.
   a. The entire discourse is given in ordinary, literal language — The choice of biblical critics.
   b. The entire discourse is figurative or metaphorical — Nobody seriously argues for this option.
   c. The discourse is partially literal and partially figurative — Virtually all evangelical Christians.
4. Eight key elements of the Olivet discourse — Ordinary or figurative language.
   a. The destruction of the temple — ordinary language.
   b. The destruction of Jerusalem — ordinary language.
   c. The coming of Christ in glory — ?
   d. The signs of the times — for the most part ordinary language.
   e. The Gospel to all nations — ?

   f. The "end of the age" — ?
   g. Astronomical upheavals — ?
   h. The term "this generation" — ?
5. The Gospel preached to all nations.
   a. The modern Christian expectation is that until the Gospel penetrates every nation Christ will not return.
   b. Several times Paul writes as if this prophecy had been fulfilled in his lifetime (cf. Rom. 10:18, 16:26; Col. 1:6, 23).
6. The end of the age — Those who believe the entire prophecy was fulfilled in 40 years believe Jesus is referring here to the end of the Jewish age and not to the end of history.
7. Astronomical upheavals
   a. In the Old Testament, it is not uncommon for prophets to describe visitations of divine judgment upon the earth by using graphic imagery very similar to Jesus' imagery in the Olivet discourse (e.g. Isa. 13:9–13; 34:3–5).
   b. These Old Testament prophecies were fulfilled without literal heavenly upheavals.
8. The main point is that something in the Olivet discourse is figurative.
9. Some say the descriptions of heavenly upheavals are figurative language, while others say the term "this generation" is figurative.

STUDY QUESTIONS

1. What is the first question that must be answered before attempting to interpret the Olivet discourse?

2. What is the difference between the popular and the proper understanding of "literal interpretation"?

3. What do the terms "ordinary" and "figurative" language mean?

4. What are the three basic options available in interpreting the Olivet discourse?

5. Which of these three options is utilized by the higher critics?

6. What are the eight key elements of the Olivet discourse that must be understood in order to interpret the text?

7. What are the elements of the Olivet discourse upon which there is virtually no disagreement?

8. What are the two possible interpretations for the phrase "end of the age"?

9. Give two examples of Old Testament prophecies of astronomical upheaval that have already been fulfilled in judgments upon specific ancient nations.

10. What is the biggest interpretive question in the Olivet discourse?

DISCUSSION QUESTIONS

1. Read Colossians 1:6 and 1:23. Discuss the implications of these statements for the interpretation of the Olivet discourse.
2. Read the following Old Testament prophecies of impending judgment upon ancient nations surrounding and including Israel. (What light is shed upon the Olivet discourse by these already fulfilled prophecies?)
   a. Babylon — Isaiah 13:9–10
   b. Egypt — Ezekiel 32:7–8
   c. Edom — Isaiah 34:4–5
   d. Israel — Amos 8:9.
3. Is it possible to interpret everything in the Olivet discourse in an absolutely literal sense without coming to the conclusion of the higher critics? What parts of the discourse do even the most literalistic evangelical interpreters see as figurative? Discuss.

5

This Generation

MESSAGE OVERVIEW

A. The Critical Phrase in the Olivet Discourse is "This Generation"
   1. The ordinary meaning of "this generation" is a reference to those people who were contemporary with Jesus.
   2. A generation is approximately 40 years.
   3. The destruction of Jerusalem and the temple did occur within 40 years of the pronouncement of this prophecy.
   4. There are several ways scholars have attempted to escape the difficulty involved here.
      a. Many argue that the escape may be found in Mark 13:32, in which Jesus qualifies His prediction.
      b. All Jesus says in verse 32 is that He cannot be more specific than He already has been about the time frame of the prophecy's fulfillment, but He certainly isn't being less specific.
      c. Others argue that the parallel statement in Matthew 16:28 was fulfilled in the Transfiguration or the Resurrection and Ascension.
      d. But Jesus' language then makes little sense because the Transfiguration took place only six days later and the Resurrection only a couple of weeks later.
      e. The most common escape hatch is to interpret "this generation" differently.
         i. Some argue that it is used to mean a kind, type or sort of person.
         ii. Some say the type of people referred to are "believers."
         iii. Others say it refers to "unbelievers."
         iv. Ridderbos argues that the term refers not to a "time frame" but a "mind frame."
      f. The problem with different interpretations such as this is that the New Testament usage of "generation" it overwhelmingly refers to the group of people alive at that time.
      g. Examples of places in the New Testament in which virtually all scholars agree that "generation" refers to the generation alive at that time: Matthew 11:16; 12:39, 41, 42, 45; 23:36; Mark 8:38; Luke 11:50–51; 17:25.

h. All of these texts point to the fact that this generation of Jews lived at a decisive point in redemptive history when God visited His people.
i. Apart from the use of "generation" in the Olivet discourse, there are 38 other uses of the word in the New Testament, and all of them refer to the contemporary group of people then alive.
j. Because of this, there must be overwhelming reasons to justify interpreting it differently.

STUDY QUESTIONS

1. What is the ordinary plain reading of Mark 13:30?
2. In what way do many scholars interpret Mark 13:32 that enables them to escape the difficulty of this passage?
3. What are the problems involved in this interpretation?
4. In what way do many scholars interpret Matthew 16:28 that enables them to escape the difficulty of this passage?
5. What are the problems involved in this interpretation?
6. What is the most common way that evangelical scholars attempt to escape the difficulty of the phrase "this generation"?
7. What is Herman Ridderbos' interpretation of "this generation"?
8. What are the problems with Ridderbos' interpretation?
9. What is the normal meaning of "generation" in its other uses in the New Testament?

DISCUSSION QUESTIONS

1. Using a concordance, find all of the uses of "generation" or "this generation" in the New Testament. How does the New Testament usage of this terminology help in understanding the Olivet discourse?
2. There are several evangelical options for understanding "this generation" in the Olivet discourse. Which option best fits the context? Why? What are the strengths and weaknesses of the different options?
3. If the term "this generation" means what it means elsewhere in the New Testament, what are some of the implications for the interpretation of the Olivet discourse? What other parts of the discourse will have to be re-examined?

6

The End of the Age

MESSAGE OVERVIEW

A. Introduction

1. Question: When Jesus spoke of His coming at the end of the age, did He mean by that the end of world history, or was He talking more specifically about the end of the Jewish age?

B. The End of the Age

1. In the New King James translation of Matthew 13:38–40, the word "world" is used in verse 38, while verses 39 and 40 use the word "age."
2. In the King James translation, all three verses use the word "world."
3. The word found in verse 38 of the Greek text is *kosmos*, which is normally translated "world," and the word found in verses 39 and 40 of the Greek text is *aion*, which means "age" or "epoch."
4. Matthew 13:38–40 refers to the end of some important time period, and the crucial question is: Which one?

C. The Times of the Gentiles

1. Luke's account of the Olivet discourse in chapter 21 of his gospel contains details not found in Matthew and Mark.
2. One of the most significant of these details is the passage referring to the "times of the Gentiles" (Luke 21:20–24).
3. Presumably the "times of the Gentiles" is differentiated from the "times of the Jews."
4. Full preterists believe all New Testament prophecies, including the final coming of Christ, the bodily resurrection of all men, and the final judgment of all men, have been fulfilled.
5. Full preterists believe that the "times of the Gentiles" was a brief period between approximately AD 69 and AD 70.

6. The problem with this position is the word "until," which refers to a terminal point — an end of the time of the Gentiles.
7. In AD 70 a period of history begins.
   a. Jerusalem was destroyed.
   b. The temple was destroyed.
   c. The Jews were dispersed.
   d. But this period of time will have a termination point in history.
8. The formation of the state of Israel in 1948 and the partial recovery of Jerusalem by the Jews in 1967 triggered more eschatological speculation than perhaps any other events in history.

D. The Fullness of the Gentiles

1. In Romans 11, Paul reveals that God is not finished with ethnic Israel.
2. There will be a future redemptive-historical action by God in relation to the Jews.
3. The Jews do not yet have complete domination of Jerusalem (e.g. the Dome of the Rock).

E. New Testament References to the Nearness of the Last Days:

1. Matthew 10:23; 26:64; Romans 13:11–12; 1 Corinthians 7:29–31; 10:11; Philippians 4:5; James 5:8–9; 1 Peter 4:7; 1 John 2:18; Revelation 1:1, 3; 3:11; 22:6–7.

F. Conclusion

1. The "Coming of Christ" referred to in these and other passages is not the final coming but Christ's judgment coming upon Israel.

STUDY QUESTIONS

1. What is the difference between the King James and the New King James translations of Matthew 13:38–40?

2. Which translation better reflects the vocabulary of the Greek text?

3. What important details are revealed in Luke's account of the Olivet discourse that are not found in Matthew's or Mark's accounts?

4. How does Luke 21:20–24 suggest the existence of a specific Jewish age?

5. How do full preterists interpret Luke 21:20–24?

6. Why is the full preterist interpretation of Luke 21:20–24 problematic?

7. What is the significance of the word "until" in this text?

8. What two twentieth century events have probably caused more eschatological speculation than any other events in history?

9. In addition to Luke 21, what other New Testament texts speak of a time of the Gentiles in contrast to a time of the Jews?

10. Name some New Testament texts that speak of the nearness of the end.

DISCUSSION QUESTIONS

1. According to full preterists, the times of the Gentiles ended in AD 70. Why is this interpretation exegetically and historically unlikely? Explain.
2. What are some possible interpretations of Romans 11 that have been suggested by biblical scholars? What are the strengths and weaknesses of each position? Which position do you believe to be the most exegetically sound? Why?
3. Read the New Testament references speaking of the nearness of the end. What are the strengths and weaknesses of the popular explanations of these texts?

7

The Destruction of Jerusalem

MESSAGE OVERVIEW

A. Introduction — Josephus

1. While we do not have an inspired biblical record of the destruction of Jerusalem, we do have a fascinating eyewitness account written by the Jewish historian Josephus.
2. In the nineteenth century, his reliability came under attack by critics who accused him of exaggeration and self-aggrandizement.

B. The Destruction of Jerusalem

1. The beginning of the end for Jerusalem came when the Roman general Vespasian invaded Palestine.
2. The Roman armies systematically invaded town after town on their way to the capital city.
3. In AD 68, Emperor Nero died and the empire was thrown into a state of tremendous conflict and even civil war.
4. Following Nero, there was a rapid succession of emperors: Galba, Otho, and then Vitellius.
5. Vitellius did not have the support of the military, which called Vespasian home to become emperor.
6. Vespasian's reign (AD 69 – 79) brought a measure of stability to the empire.
7. When Vespasian left the battlefield, he handed the leadership of the invasion over to his son Titus.
8. One of the earliest significant conflicts was the battle of Jotapata, a city governed by Josephus.
9. During the battle, over 40,000 Jews were slaughtered, but Josephus was spared and taken captive.
10. The Romans used Josephus as a negotiator and mediator during the siege of Jerusalem.

11. Josephus tried to convince the leaders of the city to surrender while also trying to convince the Romans to spare the city and the temple.

C. Significant Aspects of Josephus' Account of the Siege
   1. Like Jesus, Josephus described that generation of Jews as wicked to an unprecedented degree.
   2. Josephus describes how the Romans attacked the city by catapulting huge white stones against and over the walls.
      a. He uses the term "hailstones" to describe these weapons.
      b. As a warning the lookouts cried, "The stone cometh!"
      c. Some translations indicate that, as a way to mock the Christians, the Jews began changing this warning to, "The Son cometh!"
   3. Josephus also describes the onset of a severe famine that resulted in numerous atrocities, including cannibalism.
   4. Signs in the sky.
      a. Halley's Comet appeared in AD 66.
      b. Josephus describes an incredible phenomenon of chariots and troops appearing in the clouds around the city.
      c. He tells us that during this event, the priests heard voices saying, "Let us depart hence."
   5. According to Josephus, the destruction of Jerusalem is a divine act of vengeance by God upon His own people.

STUDY QUESTIONS

1. Who was the Jewish historian who provided us with a detailed eyewitness account of the destruction of Jerusalem?

2. What was the name of the Roman general who led the initial invasion of Palestine?

3. What were the results of Nero's suicide upon the Roman Empire?

4. Who were the three emperors who followed Nero in rapid succession?

5. Whose reign finally brought some stability to the empire?

6. Who did Vespasian leave in charge of the invasion of Palestine when he returned to Rome?

7. During what battle was Josephus captured?

8. How was Josephus used by the Romans during their siege of Jerusalem?

9. What is significant about Josephus' description of the Romans' use of catapults in their attack upon Jerusalem?

10. What were some of the signs that appeared in the skies during the siege, according to Josephus?

DISCUSSION QUESTIONS

1. Josephus' account of the destruction of Jerusalem is not inspired. How important is it, therefore, to our understanding of biblical prophecy? Explain.
2. Read selections from Josephus' *Jewish Wars*. Discuss their parallels, or lack thereof, with the New Testament prophecies of the destruction of Jerusalem.
3. Do you give any credence to Josephus' description of armies and chariots in the clouds around Jerusalem? Why or why not?

8

The Book of Revelation

MESSAGE OVERVIEW

A. Introduction — The Book of Revelation

B. When was Revelation Written?

   1. A very pressing question that is widely ignored by evangelicals is the date that Revelation was written.
   2. The majority view is that Revelation was written during the decade of the 90s during the reign of Domitian, well after the destruction of Jerusalem.
   3. But what if it was written before AD 70?
      a. This fact would help explain the language of immediacy in the book.
      b. Some scholars have argued that it was written before AD 70 with specific reference to the events surrounding the destruction of Jerusalem.

C. Dating the Book of Revelation

   1. External Evidence — Evidence found in extra-biblical writers.
      a. The strongest argument for the late date is found in the writings of the church father Irenaeus (ca. 130–202).
      b. Irenaeus wrote concerning him who beheld the apocalyptic vision, "For that was seen no very long time since, but almost in our day, towards the end of Domitian's reign."
      c. The grammatical question concerns the antecedent of the word "that" which was seen during Domitian's reign.
         i. It could refer to John's vision.
         ii. It could refer to John himself.
      d. Other relevant facts about Irenaeus' statement
         i. He also refers to "ancient copies" of Revelation, which seems incongruous with a recent vision.
         ii. He argues that all apostolic revelation ceased during the reign of Nero.

2. Internal Evidence — Evidence found in the book itself.
   a. Time-frame references — Over and over in Revelation there are time-frame references indicating the nearness of the events prophesied (cf. Rev. 1:1, 3; 3:11; 22:6–7, 10, 12, 20).
   b. Much of the symbolic language of the book is borrowed from the temple, but there is no hint that the temple is no longer standing.
   c. Revelation 17 is a critical text for dating Revelation.
      i. The text refers to seven kings: five have fallen, one is, and one has not yet come.
      ii. This raises two questions:
         1. What is the city on seven hills? In antiquity, Rome was known as the city on seven hills.
         2. Are the seven kings Roman emperors? The Jews refer to the Caesars as kings (John 19:15).
      iii. Revelation was written during the reign of the sixth king.
      iv. The first problem we face is the fact that Julius Caesar did not officially receive the title emperor.
      v. The first to officially receive the title was Caesar Augustus.
      vi. But in ancient Roman lists, Julius is listed as the first emperor.
      vii. The emperors of Rome were, according to this list:
      Julius Caesar (49–44 BC); Augustus (31–14 BC); Tiberius (14 BC–AD 37); Caligula (AD 37–41); Claudius (AD 41–54); Nero (AD 54–68); Galba (AD 68–69); Otho (AD 69); Vitellius (AD 69); Vespasian (AD 69–79).
      viii. If we start with Julius Caesar, then the sixth king is Nero.

STUDY QUESTIONS

1. What is one of the most ignored but important questions related to the book of Revelation that must be asked before one can correctly interpret it?

2. What is the majority position concerning the date Revelation was written?

3. What is the difference between external evidence and internal evidence?

4. What is the strongest piece of external evidence for the late dating of Revelation?

5. What is the significant grammatical question involved with the quotation of Irenaeus?

6. What are some of the time-frame references in the book of Revelation that point to an early date?

7. What is the significance of the temple symbolism found throughout Revelation?

8. What chapter of Revelation is especially significant for the dating of the book?

9. What city in the ancient world was known as the city on seven hills?

10. Who were the first six "kings" of the Roman Empire?

DISCUSSION QUESTIONS

1. If the book of Revelation was written prior to AD 70, how would that fact affect your interpretation of the book? Explain.
2. Discuss the external evidence for the dating of the book of Revelation. How much weight do you believe this evidence should carry? Why?
3. Discuss the internal evidence for the dating of the book of Revelation, especially the evidence in chapter 17. How much weight should be placed upon this evidence? Why?

9

The Antichrist

MESSAGE OVERVIEW

A. Introduction — The Identity of the Antichrist

B. There are several important questions surrounding the identity of the Antichrist:
   1. Is there one Antichrist or many?
   2. Is the Antichrist a person or an institution?
   3. Are the Antichrist, the Man of Lawlessness, and the Beast the same person or thing, or are they different persons or things?

C. The Antichrist
   1. 1 John 2:18ff. — In this text John speaks of antichrists (plural) and identifies them as those who have apostasized from the faith.
   2. 1 John 4:1ff. — John here speaks of something that represents a present danger to the first century church.
   3. The term *anti* in Greek has two possible meanings:
      a. It usually means "against."
      b. It sometimes means "in place of."
   4. The term antichrist, then, can mean anyone who is against Christ or a supplanter or both.

D. The Man of Lawlessness
   1. 2 Thessalonians 2:3–11 — In this text Paul tells the church that the Day of the Lord will not come until two things happen:
      a. The apostasy comes.
      b. The Man of Lawlessness is revealed.
   2. According to B.B. Warfield, the apostasy referred to here is the apostasy of the Jews in the first century.
   3. The Man of Lawlessness is described in some detail by Paul.
      a. He opposes God.

   b. He exalts himself.
   c. He sits in the temple. If this is literal, then there are two choices:
      i. It had to have occurred while the Herodian temple was still standing.
      ii. The temple must be rebuilt.
   d. The mystery of lawlessness is already at work.
   e. The Man of Lawlessness is being restrained.
   f. His coming is in accordance with the working of Satan.
4. Most scholars in the history of the church believe that the Antichrist, the Man of Lawlessness, and the Beast all refer to the same person or thing.

STUDY QUESTIONS

1. What are the three important questions raised when discussing the Antichrist?

2. What does 1 John 2:18ff. reveal about the Antichrist?

3. What does 1 John 4:1ff. reveal about the Antichrist?

4. What are the two possible meanings of the Greek word *anti* ?

5. What is the usual meaning of *anti* ?

6. What two events must occur before the Day of the Lord comes, according to 2 Thessalonians 2?

7. To which event does B.B. Warfield believe the apostasy in 2 Thessalonians 2 refers?

8. What elements of the 2 Thessalonians 2 description of the Man of Lawlessness point to a first century fulfillment?

9. Do most scholars believe that the Antichrist, Man of Lawlessness, and the Beast are the same person/thing or different persons/things?

DISCUSSION QUESTIONS

1. Many evangelical authors have pointed to specific twentieth-century figures and suggested that they may be the Antichrist spoken of in Scripture. Do 1 John 2:18ff. and 1 John 4:1ff. lend support to this type of speculation? Why or why not?
2. Second Thessalonians 2 is one of the most difficult passages in the Bible to interpret. What aspects of this chapter seem to point to a future fulfillment? What aspects seem to point to a first century fulfillment? What are some possible explanations?

3. Discuss the evidence presented in this lecture that points to Nero as the one referred to by the title the "Man of Lawlessness." Do you find this evidence persuasive? Explain.

10

The Beast

MESSAGE OVERVIEW

A. Introduction — The Beast of Revelation

B. Revelation 13 — The Vision of the Beast

1. The Beast rises out of the sea (v. 1).
2. It has seven heads and 10 horns (v. 1).
3. Its mark is the number 666 (v. 18).

C. The Mark of the Beast

1. During church history, there has been a huge amount of speculation concerning this mark.
2. Some have said that the Beast is a clergyman or a religious person of some kind.
3. During the Reformation, the most popular candidate among Protestants was the pope.
4. Others have suggested totalitarian leaders, such as Stalin, Mussolini, and Hitler.
5. In light of the many time-frame references found in Revelation, we must consider the possibility of a first century fulfillment.

D. The Case for Nero

1. Under Nero, the persecution of Christians began in a large and systematic manner.
2. Even among Pagans, no one was more distinguished for wickedness than Nero.
   a. He lived a life of violence and debauchery.
   b. He murdered his family members.
   c. He castrated and "married" a young boy.
   d. He brutally murdered his pregnant wife by kicking her to death.
   e. He devised a game in which, while clothed in animal skins, he would attack the genitals of men and women who had been tied to stakes for this purpose.
   f. The historian Tacitus spoke of his "cruel nature."

    g. Pliny referred to him as the "destroyer of the human race" and the "poison of the world."
    h. Juvenal called him a "cruel and bloody tyrant."
    i. Appolonius records for posterity the fact that the favorite nickname the people had for Nero was "the beast."
3. The number of the Beast points to Nero.
    a. In most manuscripts, the number of the Beast is recorded as 666, although in a few variant manuscripts the number is recorded as 616.
    b. Hebrew, Greek, and Latin all had systems of using letters as numbers.
    c. The name of Nero in Hebrew is *Nrwn Qsr,* which adds up to 666.
    d. Especially interesting is the fact that Nero's name in Greek, (as written in Rev. 13:18) is numerically equivalent to 616.
    e. One of the foremost textual critics of the twentieth century, Bruce Metzger, believed that this variant was intentionally inserted so Greek-speaking people could discern the identity of the beast.
4. During Nero's reign there was a rapid rise of enforced emperor worship.

STUDY QUESTIONS

1. In what chapter of Revelation do we find John's description of the Beast?

2. How does John describe the Beast?

3. What are the names of some people who at one time or another have been considered to be the Beast of Revelation 13?

4. Who was one of the most popular candidates at the time of the Reformation?

5. Who is the most likely first century candidate?

6. When did systematic persecution of the church by the Romans begin on a large scale?

7. What two great saints of the church were executed during Nero's reign?

8. What are some of the actions of Nero recorded by history that reveal his extreme wickedness?

9. What is the evidence that the number of the Beast points to Nero?

DISCUSSION QUESTIONS

1. Read Revelation 13. What characteristics of the beast out of the sea are revealed by John? What are some of the more popular interpretations of this passage found in the church today? What are some strengths and weaknesses of these interpretations?
2. In the last 50 years, prophetic authors have speculated about what the mark of the Beast is. Read Exodus 13, especially verse 9, and compare it to Revelation 13:16. How does the passage in Exodus shed light on the passage in Revelation?
3. What are the strengths and weaknesses in the argument that Nero is the "Beast" referred to in Revelation 13? Discuss.

11

The Rapture

MESSAGE OVERVIEW

A. Introduction

B. Two Types of Preterists

1. Full preterists — Believe that all biblical prophecies (including the Second Coming, the resurrection of the dead, and the Final Judgment) took place in the first century.
2. Partial preterists — Believe that although the destruction of Jerusalem in AD 70 was a return of Christ in judgment, it was not the final coming at the end of history.

C. The Resurrection of the Dead — 1 Corinthians 15:50–58

1. In the immediately preceding context, Paul speaks of believers being raised in bodies like that of Jesus.
2. In the Apostles' Creed, we affirm our faith in the resurrection of the body—not Christ's but ours.
3. Full preterists argue that this resurrection has already happened.
4. Full preterists seize upon the use of the word "we" in this passage, insisting that it must have occurred while Paul was still alive.
5. Higher critics have jumped to the same conclusion about the use of "we" in the text.
6. Paul was speaking to the Christian community then and forever, and no matter when the resurrection occurs Paul will be part of the "we."
7. The full preterist inferences are possible but not necessary.
8. Full preterists see the prophecy fulfilled in a spiritual sense in AD 70, which is a problem when discussing something physical such as a bodily resurrection.
9. This position has been charged with being a form of gnosticism because of its denial of the physical nature of the resurrection.

D. The Rapture — 1 Thessalonians 4:13–18

1. Paul is addressing a vital concern of the early church — the question of what would become of the believers who had already died.

2. Full preterists believe that this was a secret, spiritual, invisible Rapture.
3. The full preterist interpretation involves a serious bending of the words of the text.
4. Futurists, especially dispensationalists, expect the Rapture to occur before a future seven-year tribulation.
5. However, the imagery is that of Christians meeting Christ as He returns in glory.
6. It echoes the contemporary practice of the Romans.
7. When the Roman army returned victorious from battle, it would camp outside of Rome while preparations were made in the city. Then a trumpet would be blown, at which time the army would begin to march to the city, and all citizens were invited to go out to meet the army and join the march back into the city.

STUDY QUESTIONS

1. What is a full preterist?
2. What is a partial preterist?
3. What is the most significant difference between the two positions?
4. What part of 1 Corinthians 15:50–58 do full preterists seize upon in order to prove that the great resurrection occurred in the first century?
5. How do full preterists understand this prophecy to have been fulfilled?
6. What is the most significant problem with this interpretation?
7. How do full preterists interpret the Rapture text of 1 Thessalonians 4:13ff.?
8. How do dispensationalists interpret the timing of 1 Thessalonians 4:13ff.?
9. What is the contemporary first century imagery that is used by Paul in 1 Thessalonians 4?

DISCUSSION QUESTIONS

1. Read all of 1 Corinthians 15. Based upon what Paul writes here, why is the full preterist position so problematic? What are the exegetical weaknesses of the full preterist interpretation? Explain.
2. Dispensationalists cite 1 Thessalonians 4:13–18 as a major proof text for the doctrine of the pre-tribulation Rapture. Does the text mention the Tribulation? How is this fact important to the interpretation of this text?
3. Describe the practice of the Roman armies as they returned victorious from battle. In what ways does this imagery seem to influence Paul's Rapture imagery?

12

The Millennium

MESSAGE OVERVIEW

A. Introduction

B. Revelation 20 — Describes an interim period when Satan is bound and Christ is reigning with His saints

C. Amillennialism

1. Literally means "no millennium."
2. The Millennium is not a literal 1000-year period but is symbolic of the history of the church.
3. The age of the church is the age of the kingdom of God, which began with the First Advent of Christ.
4. The kingdom of God has already begun.
5. The Christian community as it manifests the kingdom will have an ongoing positive influence on culture and the human situation.
6. According to John Calvin, the supreme task of the church is to bear witness to the invisible reign of Christ, to make the invisible kingdom visible.
7. At the end of time, there will be a future apostasy and a period of great suffering — the Tribulation, in which Antichrist will become manifest.
8. At the end of this period, Christ will return and consummate all things.

D. Dispensational Premillennialism

1. The present age is the church age — a parenthetical age between the Old Testament and the millennial kingdom.
2. The coming of the kingdom is completely future.
3. There are two completely distinct programs — one for the church and one for Israel.
4. In the Millennium, the temple will be rebuilt and the sacrifices will be reinstated.
5. The church is not the new Israel and does not fulfill the Old Testament prophecies.

6. The Rapture will be followed by a seven-year Tribulation, which will end with the second coming of Christ and the establishment of the millennial kingdom.
7. At the end of the 1000-year kingdom, the final defeat of Satan will occur, along with the final judgment and the eternal state.

E. Postmillennialism

1. The church is the new Israel.
2. The kingdom of God is a kingdom of spiritual redemption.
3. Postmillennialism is the most optimistic position regarding the church's influence upon society.
4. Jesus will return at the end of a 1000-year period of great blessing.
5. For most postmillennialists, the 1000 years has not yet begun.

F. Historic Premillennialism

1. The New Testament-era church is the initial phase of Christ's kingdom.
2. The New Testament church will win occasional victories, but ultimately it will fail and become corrupt to the point of apostasy.
3. The church will pass through the Great Tribulation, at the end of which Christ will return and set up a 1000-year earthly kingdom.
4. At the end of the Millennium, Satan will be loosed and will lead a rebellion against Christ.
5. God will intervene and judge Satan; the final resurrection and judgment will then take place.

STUDY QUESTIONS

1. What is the only text in the New Testament that explicitly mentions the Millennium?

2. What period of time do amillennialists believe is represented by the 1000 years?

3. How did John Calvin understand the supreme task of the church?

4. When do amillennialists believe the kingdom of God was inaugurated?

5. How do dispensationalists understand the relationship between the church age and the millennial kingdom?

6. How do dispensationalists understand the relationship between Israel and the church?

7. What is the most distinctive feature of postmillennialism?

8. What is the most significant difference between historic premillennialism and dispensational premillennialism?

9. How do historic premillennialists understand the relationship between the church age and the millennial kingdom?

10. What millennial position is held by most partial preterists?

DISCUSSION QUESTIONS

1. Describe the basic teaching of amillennialism. What are the particular strengths and weaknesses of this position?
2. Describe the basic teaching of dispensational premillennialism. What are the particular strengths and weaknesses of this position?
3. Describe the basic teaching of postmillennialism. What are the particular strengths and weaknesses of this position?
4. Describe the basic teaching of historic premillennialism. What are the particular strengths and weaknesses of this position?